Retirement Guide

Financial Planning to Help You Retire Early & Happy

All rights Reserved. No part of this publication or the information in it may be quoted from or reproduced in any form by means such as printing, scanning, photocopying or otherwise without prior written permission of the copyright holder.

Disclaimer and Terms of Use: Effort has been made to ensure that the information in this book is accurate and complete, however, the author and the publisher do not warrant the accuracy of the information, text and graphics contained within the book due to the rapidly changing nature of science, research, the Internet, known and unknown facts. The author and the publisher do not hold any responsibility for errors, omissions or contrary interpretation of the subject matter herein. This book is presented solely for motivational and informational purposes only.

Contents

Why Don't People Plan for Their Retirement?....................1

The Basics – How Much Do I Need When I Retire?...........3

Free Money – Understanding Your 401 (k).......................11

Doing It Yourself – How An IRA Can Help You Save for Retirement...19

Catching Up – Saving for Retirement After 50................29

A Final Word of Encouragement.......................................34

Why Don't People Plan for Their Retirement?

Did you know that one-third of adult Americans recently said that they were not preparing for retirement? A recent nationwide survey conducted by financial research group Bankrate revealed that some 36% of respondents said they have not yet started saving for retirement. Even worse, more than a quarter of respondents were aged 50 to 64.

What are some of the reasons why people don't plan for retirement? The main reason is procrastination. When you are living paycheck to paycheck, it is very difficult for you to consider putting aside money. Usually they say they will wait until they get a raise before they start saving. Another reason is that their workplace does not offer a 401 (k), requiring them to go to the trouble of setting up an IRA, and most of them don't want to bother. A lot of people also say that they have no intention of retiring, since they intend to work forever.

Unfortunately, not preparing for retirement, no matter what age you are now, will cost you dearly in the future. Even if you are healthy now and intend to continue working indefinitely, you cannot expect to remain so in the long-term, since you will inevitably develop some physical ailments that will affect your ability to remain active. Even if you remain relatively healthy, can you expect that your job will still be there forever? What if you lose your job? What kind of job could you expect to get when you are past sixty or seventy? As painful as it may be, it is important to face these considerations now, while you are still earning money and able to save a nest egg that you can draw upon when and if you have decided to retire. Obviously, the early you start the better, but even at an advanced age you can still put aside enough to maintain a decent standard of living in your retirement. Even making small lifestyle changes that enable you to put some money away for the future can greatly help.

This e-book will help you start with your retirement planning by taking you through everything you need to consider, from figuring out how much you will need to maintain your desired standard of living to the best way to create a retirement portfolio that will continue to generate an income even after you have retired. Thank you for downloading my e-book and I hope that it is helpful to you!

The Basics – How Much Do I Need When I Retire?

They say that a journey of a thousand miles begins with a single step. But more important than taking that first step, however, is to have a road map that will serve as a guide to reaching your destination. Here is my suggested road map for retirement planning.

How much do you need to retire? Before you can achieve your goal, you have to define it. Computing a baseline figure of how much you will need to live on when you retire will give you an idea of how much you need to save in order to meet it. Of course, if you cannot meet your savings goal, you may have to adjust this amount so that you can live within your means.

Determine how much income you will have from sources such as Social Security or annuities. Do not include income from your investment portfolio. This is the amount that you are guaranteed to receive when you retire.

Compute the amount of your assets. These include the amount you will have in your retirement accounts (IRAs, 401 (k)) when you retire and the value of the stocks, bonds and other assets in your portfolio.

Compare this with the amount in step 1. If there is a shortfall, then this is the amount you will have to make out by increasing your savings.

Now that we've established our roadmap, we can begin our journey with the first step – how much do you need when you retire?

Computing Your Retirement Budget

Figuring out how much your expenses will be when you retire can be challenging. The most basic rule of thumb that most financial experts use is that you will need from 70% to 85% of your present salary when you retire. This assumes that you no longer have children to support and that big debts such as your mortgage will have been settled by then, allowing you to remove these expenses from your budget. You can also cut down on other expenses such as transportation and clothing since you will no longer be reporting to the office every day. Thus, if your current monthly salary is $20,000, using this guideline you will need around $14,000 to $17,000 or $168,000 to $204,000 a year.

But there are two problems with this assumption: one, it does not take into account the effect of inflation on your expenses and, two, it does not consider that you will be spending more on certain items in your budget than you do at present.

Let's look at the first issue: inflation. You probably know that prices rise over time. Generally your salary also increases to keep up with them, at least in part. But once you retire and your income becomes fixed, then you should expect that, over time, what you could easily live on today will increasingly be worth less. So you also have to take into account the effects of inflation into your savings.

Let's assume that you've decided that you need $40,000 a year to live on when you retire, in order to sustain your present standard of living. Assuming that prices rise an average of 3% a year (the historic average), then the following year, you would need $41,200, the year after that, $42,436. Ten years from retirement, you would need $52,190 to meet the same level of expenses. You would need to have saved up $458,555 just to meet your expenses for the next ten years. Of course, this is just an illustrative exercise and prices overall won't likely increase that much. But it is still clear that you will need much more down the road than you think you need now.

As for the second issue, while your overall spending may go down, there are some categories of expenses which will surely go up. The most obvious of these is, of course, health costs. Even if you are healthy now, you should expect that as you age, you will be prescribed more maintenance medication and your overall health costs will increase. And as you grow older and become more physically frail, you may need nursing care, which will be expensive. This is why you should factor health insurance into your retirement planning.

But even if you stay health and you can keep your health care costs at a minimum, other expenses may crop up to take the place of the ones that you no longer have. For example, now that you are no longer working, you may want to travel, visit their grown children and grandchildren, or even engage in volunteerism or pursue a hobby. All of these activities will take money and you may want to factor them into your planning.

The good news is that studies have shown that older adults don't sustain the same level of spending that they do in their younger years. Taking health care costs out of the equation, in general you will spend less at sixty than you did at fifty, and then less when you reach seventy and so on. But despite this caveat, most financial advisers still recommend that when it comes to retirement planning, you might want to assume that you will still have the same level of spending as you do now.

If you have a budget that you are using now, you can use this as a way to estimate more accurately how much you spend at retirement. Put this budget into a spreadsheet and use two columns – one for how much you are spending now and how much you think you will be spending at retirement. Doing this exercise allows you to see what categories of expenses you can remove when you retire. You can also add categories to this budget that you expect you will have when you retire, such as allocations for travel, the costs of your hobbies, and so on.

Apart from determining how much you will spend per year when you retire, there are two other considerations to keep in mind – when you will retire and how long you think you will live. While the general assumption is that you will retire at 65, an increasing number of people actually work past this age because they are still healthy. In fact, the mantra is that 65 is the new 45 meaning that sixty-five year old adults are generally as healthy now as forty-five year olds were in the past. In addition, if you have not started saving early enough, you will probably not be able to afford to retire at sixty-five and will need to work a few more years to make enough to sustain you.

In addition to staying healthier longer, Americans are also living longer lives in general. In 1935, the average lifespan was almost sixty-two years. Today, however, the average lifespan has increased to seventy-eight years and is reportedly continuing to increase. It is conceivable that you could live up to your late eighties or even nineties, depending on your state of health. Thus, depending on when you retire, you may need to ensure that your retirement nest egg will last you as long as thirty years.

Computing Your Social Security Benefits

Now that you have some idea of how much you will need to meet your expenses when you retire, you should look at how much you will get from Social Security when you retire. It should be noted that the mandated retirement age for Social Security is sixty-six, meaning that you are eligible for full benefits when you start drawing at this age. However, you can start availing of your benefits starting at age sixty-two, although at a reduced rate. You can also increase your benefits by delaying receiving them until you are past the mandated retirement age although you will have to start withdrawals when you reach 70.

The easiest way to determine your Social Security benefits is to look at the monthly amount that is listed under "If you continue working until you reach the full retirement age". Multiply this amount by twelve to get the full year's benefits, then multiply it by the relevant inflation factor based on how long until you retire.

Hence, if your estimated monthly benefit is $1,600 multiplied by 12 will give you a yearly benefit of $19,200. Multiply this by 1.81 and that means that your estimated yearly benefit from Social Security when you retire will be $34,752.

How Much Do I Need to Save for Retirement?

The quickest way to compute how much you need to save for retirement is to use the many online retirement calculators that are available. If you do this, we recommend that you use at least two and compare the results in order to get a more accurate idea of how much you will actually need.

You can also use the method we describe below.

The first step is to compute how much you will need per year, taking inflation into account.

Take your salary from the last working year. If you know the total amount you have spent over the last year, you can also use this figure.

Multiply this figure by the relevant inflation figure based on how long you have left until you retire. For example, if you are earning $50,000 a year and have twenty years until retirement, $50,000 x 1.81 = $90,500.

Now determine what percentage of this you will need when you retire. For example, if you decide you need 80% of your pre-retirement income then you will spend around $72,400.

Years	5	10	15	20	25	30	35	40
Inflation	1.16	1.34	1.56	1.81	2.09	2.43	2.81	3.26

Now compare the figure you get with your expected Social Security benefits. Using the example above, we see that there is a shortfall of $37,648. This is the amount that you will have to fill up with additional savings.

To estimate how much more you will have to save, take the shortfall amount and multiply it by 19.3. This multiplier figure represents the amount of savings you will have to accumulate to last 28 years assuming an average 3% inflation annually and an average annual return on your investments of six percent.

Thus, using the example above: $37,648 x 19.3 = $726,606.

Now look at how much you have currently saved. Multiply it by the growth factor based on how long you have left until retirement. This will give you the approximate worth of your savings at retirement, assuming an average return of 8% which is compounded annually.

Thus, if you have already put aside $40,000 and you still have twenty years until you retire:

$40,000 x 4.66 = $186,400

Years	5	10	15	20	25	30	35	40
Growth	1.47	2.16	3.17	4.66	6.85	10.06	14.79	21.72

Unfortunately, we can see that there is a shortfall of $540,000.

In this last step we will look at how much more you will need to put aside per year to meet your savings target and bridge the gap. Simply divide the figure by the multiplier figure based on how many more years you have to go to retire.

Years	5	10	15	20	25	30	35	40
Multiplier	6.34	15.65	29.32	49.42	78.95	122.35	186.10	279.78

Thus, $540,000/49.42 = $10,930. You will have to put aside at least $10,930 a year in order to meet your required retirement savings.

In the next section, we will look at the various investment vehicles that are available to you to save for retirement.

Free Money – Understanding Your 401 (k)

The 401 (k) is the retirement savings plan that most Americans are familiar with and are probably participating in now. It is the easiest to contribute to since contributions are taken directly from your paycheck, making saving relatively painless. Even better, in many cases, 401 (k) contributions mean 'free money' from your employer. In fact, a recent study by Fidelity Investments of 401 (k) plans that they administered revealed that of those plans that were able to save a million dollars, 28% of their balances came from employer's contributions and the interest earned on them.

401 (k) Benefits

The 401 (k) was created in 1978 by the Tax Reform Act. However, it was not until 1981 that initial regulations were finalized and taxpayers were able to save in 401 (k)'s for the first time the following year. The rules regulating 401 (k)'s were finalized and published in 1991.

The first thing to understand about a 401 (k) is that your participation is voluntary, meaning if you choose you can opt not to participate in favor of another retirement savings vehicle. It is also not mandatory for an employer to sponsor a 401 (k) plan for his employees, meaning that many workplaces may not have one. The employer can also set eligibility guidelines as to who will be allowed to participate in a company-sponsored 401 (k). For example, employees who have been with the company for less than a year may not be allowed to participate. Other categories of workers, such as part-timers and non-US citizens, may also be barred from being eligible for the plan.

The amount of your salary that you can defer to a 401 (k) plan varies from year to year based on guidelines issued by the IRS. As of 2014, the maximum amount an individual employee can contribute is $17,500 a year. In addition, if you are 50 or older as of year's end, you can make 'catch-up contributions' of a maximum $5,500.

While this may seem like a hefty amount to take out of your paycheck, the pain is ameliorated somewhat by the fact that contributions are tax-deductible. This means that your income taxes will be contributed based on the amount that is left over after your 401 (k) contributions have been taken out. For example, if you earn $60,000 a year and you choose to defer the full $17,500, your income tax will be computed based on the remaining $42,500.

As an incentive for employees to participate, the employer can also match a portion of your contributions. This matching contribution may be computed as a percentage of every dollar you contribute, i.e. the company will contribute $0.50 for every dollar you contribute, up to either a defined dollar limit or a percentage of your total salary. However, there is a limit to how much your joint contributions can be. As of 2014, the maximum amount of combined employee/employer contributions is pegged at $51,000 or $56,500 for those who are fifty or older.

Most companies may also have 'vesting' regulations. This means that only a percentage of the matching funds will belong to you if you leave the company before the vesting period is over. For example, if the vesting period is four years, only 25% may belong to you if you leave after your first year of participation, 50% in the second year, 75% in the third year and 100% after the fourth year. The company may also choose to give you the amount in full only after the full vesting period has been completed.

Choosing Your 401 (k) Investments

The plans are administered by a third-party hired by your company. These administrators may be brokerage firms such as Merrill Lynch or Schwab, insurance firms like MetLife or Prudential or mutual fund companies like Vanguard or Fidelity. These companies will invest the funds on your behalf and you will decide how you want the funds to be invested. However, it is worth noting that your choices are restricted only to those offered under your particular plan. Typically, choices consist of mutual funds, although stocks and other investment instruments can also be offered based on what is allowed under the terms of the document governing the 401(k) plan.

It is the employer who chooses which investment options to offer to employees based on what is being offered by the administrator, as well as what is in the best interests of the plan participants. In recent years, however, an increasing number of 401 (k) plans offer investment options other than those they offer as a small but vocal group of participants insisted on having a wider range of choices. If you are interested in how the employer chooses which investment vehicles to offer, ask to see your company's investment policy statement.

Here is a brief guide to the different kinds of investments that may be available to you:

Stock mutual funds. These are collections of stocks from different companies gathered together into a single fund. There are a wide variety of these stock funds that you can choose from and you should take time to familiarize yourself with them. Criteria you can use to choose include the past performance of the fund, the performance of the manager handling the fund as well as how long they've been there and how much the fund expenses are.

Bond mutual funds. Also known as managed income funds, these are mutual funds that are collections of bonds. While they are very safe investments in the sense that they generally will not experience a lot of fluctuations and will preserve your capital, they will also not generate high returns. If you are fifty and above, however, and you already are close to your target savings amount, you might want to park your money in this type of fund to preserve it and enjoy modest gains.

Target-date funds. If you are interested in a low-maintenance way to invest, you can choose this type of fund. Simply pick the fund whose target-year is the year that you retire. The asset allocation of the fund will be automatically adjusted year-by-year as the target date approaches. You can also choose among different risk levels – conservative, moderate or aggressive – and you can change your risk level as your risk tolerance changes and your retirement date approaches. For example, if you are close to retirement and you are not yet close to your target amount, you might want to shift from moderate to aggressive. Criteria you can choose for picking target-date funds include the strength of its underlying holdings, its glide path (the formula it uses to create its asset allocation mix) and the fees it charges.

Blended funds. These are funds that combine stocks and bonds in a set allocation, i.e. 50% stocks to 50% bonds or 70% stocks to 30% bonds.

Choosing which funds to put your money in depends on what age you are, how far you are from retirement and how much you have already saved. The younger you are, the more of your money you should put in funds that generate high returns, such as stocks. One rule of thumb you can use is to subtract your age from 100 and then use that as a basis for allocating stock funds in your portfolio. Thus, if you are currently 40, you should put 60% of your money into stock funds. However, if you are more aggressive and want to maximize your returns, you can increase this allocation.

You can also choose the above formula to choose a blended fund. In the example above, you can pick a blended fund that has 60% stocks and 40% funds. But if you are opting for a blended fund, you should also look at the fees they charge since they can affect your returns.

Withdrawing From Your 401 (k)

You can start making withdrawals from your 401 (k) as early as when you reach 59.5 years of age. However, mandatory withdrawals start at 70.5. This means that when you reach 59.5 you can start making withdrawals but are not required to. However, when you reach 70.5 you must start withdrawing from your 401 (k) and you cannot just leave the funds in the plan to continue growing. You are exempted from this requirement if you are still employed at 70.5 and the terms of your plan allow you to defer required minimum distributions.

If you withdraw from your 401 (k) before you reach the mandated 59.5 years, you will be levied a 10% early distribution penalty. And since the funds you withdraw will be treated as ordinary income you risk losing your tax benefit as well. However, if you experience a hardship and your plan allows hardship withdrawals, you can take money out early from your plan. It should be noted that not all plans allow hardship withdrawals and these can be made only under stringent conditions, such as if you need immediate funds to meet a heavy financial need and there is no other way to meet it. The withdrawals are also subject to the 10% penalty and will be subject to income tax, but you do not have to pay the amount back into your plan. Once you withdraw, you cannot make another contribution to your plan for the next six months.

If you need money badly, however, there is an alternative to early withdrawal – taking out a loan against your 401 (k). Again, this option is only available if the employer chooses to allow employees to do so. If loans are allowed, you can borrow up to 50% of your vested balance, up to a maximum $50,000. The repayment term is generally five years but if the loan is used to purchase a primary residence it may be longer. The interest charged on the loan is required to be in line with that charged by financial institutions for comparable loans.

How much will you pay in taxes when you start making withdrawals from your 401 (k)? It depends on what your tax bracket is when you retire, which in turn, is determined by the amount of income you have when you retire.

Changing Jobs

If you move to another workplace, you have a number of options as to how to handle your 401(k). If your employer allows it, you can leave the balance there and allow it to grow even though you will not be allowed to make new contributions. However, if the amount falls below a certain threshold, you may be required to cash out or roll it over.

If there is a 401 (k) plan at your new workplace, you can roll it over to the new plan. Before you do so, however, you should compare the expenses and fees of the old and new plans to see whether it is more beneficial to move or leave the funds in the old plan.

You can also roll over the funds to a traditional or Roth IRA. This is a good option if your new workplace does not have a 401 (k) since it allows you to continue saving toward your retirement. Since you are not participating in a retirement plan in your workplace, you can also enjoy the full range of tax benefits as described in the next section.

One thing you should avoid doing, however, is to cash out your 401 (k). While cashing out seems like an easy solution to dealing with your 401 (k) when changing jobs, it can adversely affect your retirement savings. Even a seemingly small amount such as $5,500 can greatly increase to as much as $58,700 when left to grow in an IRA for thirty-five years.

Cashing out also has serious tax implications. Twenty percent of the balance is automatically withheld by the plan administrator in order to cover any taxes you may owe to the IRS. If you're below 59.5, you also face a 10% early withdrawal penalty if you cash out. This means that a big chunk of your money will go to the IRS before it ever reaches you.

Doing It Yourself – How An IRA Can Help You Save for Retirement

Since we've already established that a lot of Americans don't save for retirement, it should not surprise you that a lot of Americans who are aware of their options for retirement savings spend less time thinking about them than about which restaurant they will go to for their anniversaries. According to the 2014 IRA survey by financial services organization TIAA-CREF, one-fourth of respondents spent two hours or more deciding which restaurant to go to for a special occasion while only fifteen percent spent the same time planning their IRA investment.

In addition, one-third or 35% of respondents did not understand what an Investment Retirement Account

(IRA) was or what benefits it offered compared with a 401 (k). Even worse, 45% of the younger respondents aged 18 to 34 who would benefit most from already starting to put away money for retirement said they did not understand IRAs.

Of course, if you are already contributing to a 401 (k) in your workplace, it should not be surprising that you do not care about exploring other retirement savings options. After all, you probably feel that you are already contributing enough towards your retirement. In fact, 46% of respondents said that they don't earn enough to save more than they are already putting away.

Even if you have a 401 (k) in your workplace, you should still look into investment retirement accounts. If you started saving for retirement at a later age, an IRA can help you meet your savings goal and ensure a comfortable retirement. If you don't have access to a 401 (k), an IRA can ensure that you are saving enough to provide for yourself when you stop working.

There are two types of IRAs that you can set up as an individual taxpayer saving for retirement – the traditional and the Roth IRA.

Traditional IRAs

An IRA is a self-funded requirement account that works similarly to a 401 (k). The main difference is that it is your responsibility to open an IRA and to fund it. Any person, or their spouse if married, who earned taxable compensation during the year can open and fund a traditional IRA provided they did not reach the age of

70.5 by the end of the year. In addition, if both spouses are earning taxable compensation, they can each open an IRA.

For 2014 and 2015, annual contribution limits are set at 100% of compensation up to $5,500 and if you are 50 and above you can contribute an additional $1,000 for a total of $6,500. However, if you 'roll over' or deposit pre-retirement payments into your IRA from another retirement account such as a 401 (k) or another IRA, these limits do not apply.

However, if one spouse is not earning income or has a small income, the working spouse can make contributions to an IRA on their behalf. This special type of IRA is called a spousal IRA and is the exception to the rule that a non-working person cannot fund an IRA. A spousal IRA is not a joint account since all IRAs, by definition, must be held individually. You qualify to open a spousal IRA if you file a joint return with your spouse and have earned income that is at least the value of the annual contribution you make to your IRAs.

The same contribution limits apply to spousal IRAs as regular IRAs. Thus, if the working spouse contributes $5,500 ($6,500 if they are 50 and up) to their IRA, they can contribute up to $5,500 ($6,500 if the spouse is aged 50 upwards) to a spousal IRA, allowing the family to jointly contribute as much as $11,000 ($13,000 if both spouses are above 50). The amount of the allowable contribution to a spousal IRA is determined by the combined gross income of both spouses less the contribution of the spouse with the higher income to a traditional IRA and any contribution they make to a Roth IRA for their spouse.

Same-sex couples living in states that recognize same-sex marriages generally should be allowed to open spousal IRAs but some legal problems may arise if the state does not call the union a 'marriage' but just a 'recognized domestic partnership' or 'civil union'.

You can open an IRA even if you already have a 401 (k) or other retirement account; however, having another retirement plan can determine whether or not you are eligible for tax deductions. If you are not covered by a retirement plan than you can deduct your contributions in full; if you are, then the following guidelines apply based on your adjusted gross income and filing status:

Full deduction up to contribution limit: $60,000 or less (single or head of household); $96,000 below (married but filing jointly or qualified widow/widower).

Partial deduction: over $60,000 but below $70,000 (single or head of household); over $96,000 but less than $116,000 (married but filing jointly or qualified widow/widower); below $10,000 (married but filing separately).

No deduction: over $70,000 (single or head of household); above $116,000 (married but filing jointly or qualified widow/widower); $10,000 and above (married but filing separately).

You can open an IRA at a bank, mutual fund, life insurance provider or other financial institution, or with a stockbroker. Contributions to the IRA must be made in cash.

One of the major benefits of an IRA is that you have more leeway as to what investments you can make. Unlike a 401 (k) where you are limited only to the choices offered by the sponsor of the fund, you can basically choose any investment asset that you want subject to IRS restrictions.

What are not allowed as IRA investment assets? The main restriction made by the IRS is that you are prohibited from investing in collectibles, including rare coins and stamps, valuable artwork, jewelry, wines and precious metals (with certain exceptions).

In addition, the trustee holding your IRA is allowed to impose additional restrictions on allowable investments. For example, although the IRS does not specifically prohibit investments in real estate, the trustee may choose to disallow it due to the administrative difficulties of holding this asset.

You can also choose certain precious metals such as gold, platinum and silver as your investment provided they fall within IRS guidelines. Allowable gold, silver and platinum assets must be at least 99.99% pure and be in the form of gold coins or bullion bars. Coins that can be held as IRA assets include the US Gold Eagle, US Silver Eagle, US Platinum Eagle and Canadian Gold Maple Leaf while coins such as the South American Krugerrand are not allowed. These assets must be held by the trustee and not the owner.

When you reach 70.5 you are required to start receiving distributions from your IRA. If you do not start taking distributions by April 1 of the year following the year in which you reached this age, you risk paying a 50% excise tax on the amount that should have been distributed. Thus, if you turn 70.5 in 2014, you must start taking distributions by April 1 of 2015.

The amount of the required minimum distribution is computed based on your age on your birthday this year divided by the distribution period. For example, if you are seventy this year, your required minimum distribution is your IRA balance as of December 31 of the following year divided by 27.4. There is a worksheet you can download from the IRS website that you can use to compute your RMDs. However, a different computation is used for IRA owners who have a spouse that is over ten years younger and is their sole beneficiary for the account. These withdrawals are taxed as regular income based on your tax bracket at the year the withdrawal is made.

However, if you need to you can start taking out money from your traditional IRA when you reach 59.5, which will be taxed as if it were ordinary income. If you need to take out money before 59.5 you can do so provided it falls under the following qualifying reasons:

Paying college expenses for yourself or your spouse, your children and your grandchildren.

Paying for medical expenses that exceed 7.5% of your AGI (adjusted gross income).

Paying for a first-time house purchase up to a $10,000 limit.

Paying for the expenses of a sudden disability.

If you need money you can also take back one contribution to your traditional IRA without being levied a penalty. However, the withdrawal should be made before the tax deadline of the year and the amount is not deducted from your taxes.

You can also inherit an IRA as a beneficiary. In this case, you can choose to designate yourself as the owner of the inherited IRA, roll it over into your own IRA or another retirement account such as a 401 (k) or treating yourself as the beneficiary. In the latter case, you can set up an IRA in the name of the deceased and make a trustee-to-trustee transfer of the funds to it. You cannot make contributions to it but must start receiving distributions from it at 70.5 as the beneficiary.

Roth IRA

A Roth IRA is like a mirror image of a traditional IRA in that contributions are not tax-deductible but your withdrawals are tax-free. You can contribute to a Roth IRA if your taxable compensation and modified adjusted gross income (AGI) is below $188,000 for married couples filing a joint return or a qualifying widow or widower, less than $127,000 for single taxpayers or those with head of the household status or married taxpayers who are filing a separate return provided they did not live off the income of their spouse at any time during the year you filed and below $10,000 for a married taxpayer who is filing a separate return and lived with his or her spouse at any time during the year you filed.

As with a traditional IRA, you can contribute up to $5,500 annually for 2014 and 2o15. If you are age fifty and above, you can contribute an additional $1,000 for a total $6,500 annual contribution. According to Roth IRA guidelines, however, the deadline for making a contribution is fifteen months from the current taxable year. Thus, if you are making a contribution for tax year 2014 is by April 15, 2015. You can contribute at any time before this deadline.

There are two more benefits that you can enjoy with a Roth IRA as opposed to a traditional IRA. You can continue making contributions to your Roth IRA even past 70.5, and you are not required to take mandatory distributions when you reach 70.5. You can leave the funds in the account for as long as you wish and they will continue growing on a tax-free basis. And withdrawals made between 59.5 and 70.5 are not taxed since they are treated as normal retirement income

However, you can start taking contributions out of your Roth IRA account at any time as long as you've had the account for at least five years. But removing investment earnings is prohibited until you reach the age of 59.5 unless there is a qualifying reason which is the same as those for traditional IRAs.

Which is Right for Me?

If you have a 401 (k) plan at work and your employer generously matches it, you should make sure to contribute the maximum amount first to take advantage of the match before you fund an IRA. Once you've made the full allowable contribution to your 401 (k) and you are still able to put aside money in an IRA, here are some of the considerations to keep in mind when choosing between a traditional and Roth IRA:

Will you still have other sources of income when you retire? If you anticipate that you won't need the money when you hit 70.5, then a Roth IRA allows you to keep it in the account to continue growing tax-free.

If you won't have other sources of income and you think that you'll be in a lower tax bracket when you retire, a traditional IRA may be more beneficial. Since your contributions are deductible and you'll only be paying taxes once you start taking out withdrawals at 59.5 or 70.5, you may ultimately end up with a lower tax bill, depending on when you choose to start withdrawing.

If you want more flexibility with regards to access to your money, then a Roth IRA may be a better choice. You can withdraw your contributions at any time after you've had your account for five years, but you have to leave your investment earnings in the account until you reach 70.5 or pay taxes on them.

If you anticipate that the long-term capital gains tax will increase then a Roth IRA is the better choice. With a traditional IRA, all distributions when you retire will be taxed as ordinary income, whose rate is higher than the capital gains tax at present.

If you are starting to make contributions to an IRA at a young age and you anticipate that you will earn more in the future and move to a higher tax bracket, then a Roth IRA is the better choice.

If your retirement is already spoken for and you would like to leave behind some money for your heirs, then a Roth IRA is the perfect vehicle. Not only will the money in the account grow tax-free, it can remain in the account indefinitely since you are not required to take mandatory distributions. And you can bypass the capital gains taxes on investments such as stocks and bonds that generate income or appreciate in value.

Catching Up – Saving for Retirement After 50

Even if you have not yet started putting aside money for retirement or still have a long way to go before you meet your savings goals, it is not too late! There are many strategies that you can adopt that will help you save for retirement. Keep in mind that assuming that you work until you're sixty-five or seventy, you still have a lot of time before you have to start drawing on your retirement savings

At this point, however, you should probably keep your expectations realistic. You will probably not be able to save as much as you would have if you had started even ten years earlier. You may need to downsize your lifestyle when you retire. But you can still have a comfortable retirement but just not the one that you might have envisioned.

Another thing you will have to accept is that you will need to make sacrifices now to ensure your future in the long-term. There are some things that you may have to give up in order to free money for savings. You may have to put off vacations and spending for big-ticket items. But you need to take the longer view. You don't want to run out of money when you are old and can no longer work. It would also be difficult at an advanced age for you to take on a minimum wage job such as greeter at a Wal-Mart or working at a McDonalds.

The first step in catching up is to take full advantage of the increased contributions you can make to your 401 (k) or IRA. If you haven't been contributing enough to your 401 (k) to take advantage of the company match, if there is one, then you should start adding to your contributions.

You should also explore opening a Health Savings Account. If you are currently participating in a high-deductible health plan, you are eligible to make contributions to an HSA. As of 2014, you can contribute up to $3,300 for individual coverage and $6,550 for families, plus an additional $1,000 for taxpayers who are already 55 and above at the start of the current tax year.

Contributions made to an HSA are tax-deductible on your gross income provided you make them with after-tax dollars. Earnings generated from the assets in the form of interest or other income is also tax-free. Once the HSA is funded you can make withdrawals from them without paying Federal or state income taxes provided they are used for qualified medical expenses as detailed in the IRS Publication 502. And any money left over from your account is rolled over to the following year.

You should also look into taking out long-term insurance when you reach your sixties, particularly if you have health concerns. This type of insurance pays for the costs of a nursing home stay or twenty-four hour care at home, which is very expensive and can easily deplete your retirement savings.

However, premiums can be expensive so you should consider if your budget can afford it. Keep in mind that you may need to pay premiums for years before you need to claim benefits. To save on premiums, instead of opting for lifetime coverage starting from when you need nursing home care, consider just covering yourself for a particular period, such as five years, since it is not likely that you will stay in a nursing home for a long period. You can also reduce premiums by adding a waiting period of around 90 to 120 days. But to ensure that your policy can keep up with rising health care costs, look for one with an inflation rider provision.

Another good strategy to prepare for retirement is to pay off big debt such as your mortgage now so that you won't have to deal with them later, when you have no income except for your savings. If you cannot pay them off completely, you can refinance and pay off as much as you can now so that you can only pay the minimum after retirement. Adopt the same strategy with your car loan.

Credit card debt is another issue you will have to address before you retire. Create a strategy to start paying off your consumer debt, starting with the card that charges the highest interest rate. If you have no credit card debt, then you should look at the finance charges of the card or cards you currently have, and consider dropping the ones which charge high interest rates and fees for ones that are more affordable.

You should also consider downsizing options for when you retire. For example, once the children have started their own families, you can look into moving into a smaller house to lower your expenses. You can also start looking into disposing of big items that you may no longer need after you retire, such as an extra car.

You will also have to look into ways you can save money. For example, you can switch to a more affordable cell phone service provider. Look for one that provides just the services that you need and does not charge you extra for additional features such as unlimited text messaging or hundreds of call minutes. You can also look for a plan that charges you on a post-paid basis so you'll only be paying for what you actually use.

You may also qualify for discounts on your auto insurance, particularly if you sell your expensive car and opt for a cheaper used one that will be more affordable to insure. And if you spend a lot on gas when you are traveling, you can consider apps such as GasBuddy to help you save on fuel costs.

Speaking of insurance, you should reconsider your life insurance policy, particularly if your children are self-sufficient financially and do not need the death benefits as badly. Even if you decide you still need life insurance coverage, you can opt for a cheaper policy.

If you have marketable skills or entrepreneurial acumen, you can consider generating more income by starting a home-based business. If it takes off, it can help you in your retirement years by continuing to be a source of income for you, as well as helping keep you active and engaged so you won't atrophy mentally.

Another strategy you need to look into is becoming more aggressive in your investments. You may need to increase your exposure to higher-risk investments such as stocks that will potentially give you higher returns. You might want to consider consulting with a professional financial planner who works on a fee-only basis to help you decide the best way to maximize your returns on your investment portfolio.

Finally, you can consider delaying retirement. Instead of retiring at sixty-five, you can retire at seventy. This will not only extend the time you are pulling down an income, it will also give more time for the money in your retirement accounts to grow tax-free. It will also help increase your Social Security benefits. Or you can work part-time after you retire so that you would continue to pull in income.

A Final Word of Encouragement

Even if you started saving late, you can still save enough to give yourself a comfortable retirement. If you make sure you set realistic goals and then dedicate yourself towards meeting them. Let's face it, with the times being as hard as they are and our salaries seemingly not enough to make ends meet, savings can easily be pushed down on our list of priorities. But we should always prioritize savings since this is the only way that we can protect ourselves from economic reversals and ensure our future.

It would probably greatly help you if you changed your attitude towards saving. Instead of seeing it as a sacrifice that deprives of you some of the simple joys of life, you should look at it as a voluntary step you are taking towards meeting your goal. Each dollar you succeed in putting aside in a retirement account puts you closer towards a future in which you can spend your retirement years doing just what you want to do and pursuing hobbies and other interests that you never had time to do when you still had to work full-time.

Thank you again for downloading this e-book! If you enjoyed it, please take the time to share your thoughts and post a review on Amazon. It'd be greatly appreciated!

Thank you and good luck!

www.ingramcontent.com/pod-product-compliance
Lightning Source LLC
Chambersburg PA
CBHW051825170526
45167CB00005B/2159